DELIVERANCE
from
FEAR

ELISA RENDON

WESTBOW
PRESS®
A DIVISION OF THOMAS NELSON
& ZONDERVAN

WestBow Press books may be ordered through booksellers or by contacting:

WestBow Press
A Division of Thomas Nelson & Zondervan
1663 Liberty Drive
Bloomington, IN 47403
www.westbowpress.com
844-714-3454

ISBN: 978-1-6642-5069-7 (sc)
ISBN: 978-1-6642-5068-0 (e)

Library of Congress Control Number: 2021923748

Print information available on the last page.

WestBow Press rev. date: 12/22/2021

PART 1

I n our walk with the Lord Jesus, we often encounter situations we do not know how to solve. Our own mistakes in doing, thinking, and saying things that are counterproductive to our Christian journey cause difficulties when we try to follow the Lord's will. There is no such thing as a perfect Christian. There are redeemed Christians. It is hugely important to understand this difference. We all make mistakes. We do and say things that are harmful to ourselves and others and go astray from the path that God has prepared for us.

When we give our hearts to Jesus, we know that we have a Savior and a supreme priest who will plead our cause before the Father. Before leaving the earth, he told his disciples that he would be sending the Holy Spirit to comfort and guide us (John 14:16 KJV). When Jesus came to the earth, he came in a human body. He could feel as we did, suffer as we did, and understand our weaknesses. We have a Savior who underwent the most atrocious torture and death so we could be redeemed from our sins.

As a teenager, I gave my heart to Jesus. But events took place in the congregation where I was that shook me, and I was driven away. For many years I lived a life of sin by following my desires, although deep inside, I continued searching. This culminated in an illicit relationship while being married when my daughter was eighteen months old. I became involved in Santeria, a practice that involves being the conduit of and serving the spirits of the dead. This practice is commonly found in Hispanic countries and dates from the time the African people were brought to the New World. In order to continue worshiping their pagan gods, the founders of this practice named the spirits after the Catholic saints and the Virgin Mary.

When my husband became aware of this relationship, he was relentless in his anger. I took an overdose of pills and was in a hospital ward for several days. The one good thing that came out of this situation was the lady who my husband hired to look after me and go everywhere with me was an evangelical Christian. We became close friends, and she brought me back to the Lord. I went through my home looking for everything I could give her that was in some way against the Christian faith and worship.

With her guidance, I began reading the scriptures once again, and the Holy Spirit once more came to dwell inside me. I began praying in earnest, through many years, that my son and my daughter would give their hearts to Jesus. For my son, this happened when he was beginning high school, but then he went astray. I had begun teaching my daughter how to pray once she was old enough to understand the meaning of her prayers. We prayed together, and she read to me passages from the scriptures. My son came back to the Lord in a way I did not expect. He enlisted in the army and was stationed at Fort Brun, near the Canadian border. There he found a church, the Calvary Chapel, and gave his heart to Jesus once again.

My marriage has been difficult, as my husband never forgave me for falling in love with another man. Our relationship is very strained. My daughter, son, and I pray for him to be saved and born again. I have mental disorders. When I have a crisis, my daughter puts Christian music on YouTube for me to listen to. As scriptures say, "He dwells in the praises of His children" (Psalm 22:3 KJV). Throughout the years, I have learned a lot about how the Lord does his work. Many times I have asked to be healed from my mental illness, but his answer has been to direct me to the words he told the apostle Paul. "Be glad of your infirmities, because in your weakness I am glorified" (2 Corinthians 12:9 KJV).

My daughter and I are unable to attend an evangelical congregation as my husband is Catholic and he believes evangelicals are out of the church. I have nurtured myself throughout the years with Christian music, books, and scriptures. I have received the prayers of countless people whom I have not met but who I know the Lord has given the task of interceding for our family. Walking with Jesus is a journey of learning and discovery. In order to truly worship him, "in Spirit and in truth" (John 4:23–24 NKJV), we must delve into the deepest parts of ourselves and search for the things that need to be removed, healed, or made anew. The Holy Spirit helps us in this journey and goes into our innermost being, to our very entrails, to uproot negative traits and instill those that may be used to fulfill the will of God.

Our walk with the Lord is meant to be a deep, intimate journey where we are guided into discovering what are the things that he wants us to do. Fulfilling the will of God and carrying the message of salvation to all places are the two most important tasks he gives us. His desire is that "none perish, but many may come to repentance" (2 Peter 3:9 NIV-MIT).

How can I fulfill his will in my life? He has given me this skill of writing. Therefore, I put it to his service and as an instrument of carrying his Word throughout the world. Intercessory prayer is the other task I feel that he has entrusted with me. I am glad and grateful that I can use my skill of writing for his glory and to help the Word of salvation get spread further.

God has entrusted us with a special mission. Jesus said to his disciples, "Once you receive power, you are to go and tell the good news of the Gospel to all nations" (Mark 16:15 ISV). We are to spread the Word to all corners of the world. Following through with this mission is sometimes difficult. I found Jesus as a teenager. There were serious problems in the church I attended for seven years, and I fled in pain. It took several years before I found my way back to the Lord, and I encountered a great deal of pain as a result of doing things my own way.

At twenty-six years of age, I was diagnosed with paranoid schizophrenia, a diagnosis that would later change to schizoaffective disorder. I asked only one thing of the doctor who attended me: for him not to put me in the hospital. He agreed and said in turn I was to take the medications he prescribed for me. It was a long, painful summer. My doctor had to experiment with different medicines before he found the right combination to give me because I was also diagnosed with depression.

We each kept our end of the bargain. In September I was able to return to work. This was both positive and scary. I feared that people would probe in order to find out what exactly was wrong. This was thirty-three years ago, and the stigma against mental illness was much stronger than it is today. There was another problem, one that would plague me throughout my working life. The medications I was taking made me very sleepy; I struggled to make it to work every morning.

I had an untold number of meetings with my supervisor and her manager. It was exhausting and painful. Most importantly, it was something beyond my control. I tried going to bed earlier, but the struggle to get up when the alarm rang was staggering. I managed to continue working and not get dismissed, but as different people became supervisors, the issue continued to come up. The fact that the stigma was true continued to materialize in the lack of empathy and understanding by any supervisor I had. At best, I had to pretend that I did not hear comments exchanged, which highlighted my lateness and absenteeism. At worst, paranoid thoughts raced through my mind each working day, haunting me with jeers and cackles.

As the years progressed, a new issue emerged. Every year, I had to go on sick leave for three months. It was the only way I could remain working. During one of those leaves, the manager called me and said that if I did not return to work by a specified date, I would lose my job. Every time I returned to work, I felt worse in the atmosphere I was functioning in. I began to experience bouts of anxiety and panic attacks. Five years before I resigned, I started developing chronic headaches, which were eventually diagnosed as migraines.

I resigned from the staff position as an interpreter and began working as a freelance interpreter. My work life and I parted ways one autumn day when I got home from working in one of the courts. It was something that took on nightmarish qualities. I took an overdose and survived, but it left me reeling and unable to process the changes I was experiencing. My doctor filled out the necessary papers, and six weeks later, the decision came from the government.

I was declared disabled, and I began receiving benefits after a period of six months, which was mandated by law. That was the only thing that was easy. I stopped hearing from former colleagues and faced an untold world of loneliness and grief. I had no one to talk to but my doctor and my mother. My one joy, my saving grace, was my little son, who was about to turn five at that time. His giddiness and antics made me feel alive and thankfully not stigmatized.

When my son started attending school, new issues arose. I was not working, but I was unable to attend PTA meetings, bake cookies for fundraising events, and attend celebrations like other mothers. I did manage to always celebrate his birthday in class by bringing cupcakes and juices and having his classmates sing happy birthday to him. I tried to give him as normal a life as I could by taking him to the park and Chuck E. Cheese and reading him books.

As I turned forty, something happened that I was later able to see as God's intervention. Although I was using contraceptives, I found out I was again expecting. My first reaction was to break down in tears. I didn't know how I would be able to raise another child. My marriage was going through rough times, and I was afraid of the effects my medicines would have on the fetus.

Because of the medicines, I was referred for genetic counseling. The lady I spoke to was a wonderful, caring person. She laid out reality very matter-of-factly. What she told me was that I needed the medications in order to function normally, so I had to keep on taking them to be there for my baby. My doctor changed some of the medications to similar ones that had undergone greater research and were determined to be safe for the fetus.

Although I had not gone back to Jesus, I can see how his hand was over the pregnancy. I had an early amniocentesis and found out the baby would be a girl. That cheered me up, and I began dreaming about little outfits. My neighbor's wife, a wonderful young woman who also had a little girl, gave me two boxes of perfectly folded clothes that were beautiful. Then one of her friends also sent me another box with lovely, little outfits. Also, my mother and I would go to the stores, and although I only bought three or four pieces, I really enjoyed those outings.

As part of the monitoring over the pregnancy, I had to go for several ultrasounds, and it was during one of those times that the technician mentioned that because the liquid in the amniotic sac was always low, I should drink more water. She told me to drink a gallon of water a day, and I started to do so. At seven and a half months of pregnancy, I was admitted to the hospital with high blood pressure. When my discharge was to take place, another ultrasound was taken, and it was found the amniotic fluid was low. It was determined I was to undergo an early C-section, and I was transferred to another hospital that had a neonatal intensive care unit. I arrived there early evening on December 31, 2003. Shortly after my arrival, I had congestive heart failure.

A cardiologist and a pulmonologist were brought in, and the cardiologist contacted the director of the department of congestive heart failure in the hospital. From what I was told, as little by little I pieced together the details, he said I had twenty pounds of extra water in my body and to survive, ten would need to be extracted. Since I was drinking such a large amount of water, my kidneys could not process it, and the water was around the pericardium and had gone into the lungs.

Once the ten pounds were drained, another ultrasound was performed. The liquid in the amniotic sac had dropped too much and a C-section was scheduled for the following Monday, early in the morning. My daughter was born weighing three pounds and eight ounces. She was in NICU for five weeks, and I was an inpatient for three weeks. I received additional treatment for the congestive heart failure and was discharged in good condition. I followed up with treatment for a month, until the fluid level returned to normal.

We visited the baby every day, but only my husband and I were able to go in, so my son watched from the outside. The baby gained ounces little by little and learned to suck formula from a tiny tube, since my medicines would pass through the breast milk. Once she learned to drink the formula, we were able to bring her home. All throughout, my son's joy was infectious. As I look back to that time, I see how the Lord orchestrated everything that happened; it would not be for another two years that I gave my life back to Jesus, when a Christian lady was brought to the house to care for me, following another overdose.

This was a significant circumstance because I had become friends with the father of one of my son's classmates and had been initiated into Santeria. Santeria is a practice notorious in the Caribbean, although it is also practiced in other Spanish-speaking countries. This practice spanned from the Yoruba religion of the African slaves who had been brought to the New World. In order to avoid persecution by the Spaniards, they adopted the Catholic saints and the Virgin Mary and gave them their ancestral names.

This is a practice of the occult, and I was found by my mentor, whom I had fallen in love with, to be a gifted medium, since I was an excellent conduit for all the spirits. Shortly before Christmas, a confrontation with my husband erupted. He had found in my cell phone the number of my mentor and demanded to know why we were calling each other. During the exchange, he grabbed the beads I wore around my neck, symbolic of my patron spirit, and tore them off.

Since my way of dealing with distress always led to suicidal thoughts, I took another overdose and survived it. It was then that the evangelical Christian lady was brought into my house to care for me, and she was God's conduit to bring me back to him. When she explained to me the significance of all the objects I had been given, as well as the fact that idolatry is abominable to God, I began going through the entire house, giving her everything I could find that could remotely be associated with the occult.

Since coming back to Jesus, I found, most of all, his grace and mercy. I continued to have a troubled marriage in the years to come but being able to stay at home with my daughter, something I had been unable to do with my son, was a great joy. Granted, the issues that were present when my son was little came back as she grew. I took her to the park and to the swings, but socializing with other moms was impossible.

Once she began school, I continued bringing in cupcakes and juices for birthday parties in her class, but I learned painfully that volunteering was not a good idea. I found myself one day standing in the middle of the library, where I had been assigned, because it was the book fair and children would be coming in to purchase books and other items, and the feeling of vulnerability must have been written on my forehead with neon letters because I saw two mothers looking at me with pity.

I was able to do birthday parties at home and invite the girls who were her friends. These parties were successful because they basically wanted to have fun and turned the house upside down. We always ordered pizza to go with the cake and juice, and I allowed them to run around and just enjoy themselves, and afterward I cleaned up and organized the house. All throughout this time, I keenly felt the absence of friends. There was one woman whom I had been able to befriend, a very compassionate person, but she moved away.

My efforts to make friends were hampered by my issues of inadequacy and the perennial inclusion of the paranoia. However, because I had come back to Jesus, I was able to call upon his name when I felt distress. When my daughter was old enough, I taught her how to pray. I also told her, as I had told my son, when each of them was old enough to understand, that if they saw their mom cry or scream, it was not because they had done something wrong but because mom had an illness.

My one prayer, once I came back to Jesus, was that my children would become believers and would be saved. I also prayed that they would not suffer from paranoia. God, in his mercy, answered my prayers. My son gave his heart to Jesus when he was stationed with the army nearby a church that taught the gospel and prayed to Jesus as the intercessor and High Priest. My daughter began praying with me, and in many instances that I have been in crisis situations, she has pleaded with the Lord for deliverance.

I believe the Lord blessed them and sealed them with his Spirit. They also have been blessed with robust self-esteem. I believe the Lord gave me these children because he knew how hard the impact of my mother becoming ill with Alzheimer's and dementia would be on me. My mother had been throughout my life my friend as well as mother, and her love was unwavering. When she became ill, she had to be put in a nursing home because my house has the bedrooms on the second floor, and she was eventually bound to a wheelchair, which made it unable for her to be in the bedrooms upstairs.

This circumstance caused me much pain and guilt, and Jesus lovingly held me through the years she was in the nursing home until she passed away. I once again thanked Jesus for my children because having to raise my daughter gave me strength and comfort. Her delightful laugh, which would leave everyone else laughing, was a balm for my pain. With the passing of time, I continued to feel the loss of my mother acutely. Her presence, throughout my illness, had been a place of solace and support.

In an effort to return to work, I went for vocational rehabilitation. I took a course as a medical assistant in the hopes of being able to care for my mother, but that never materialized. I became employed as a greeter in the emergency room of a regional hospital, working a part-time shift every weekend. This allowed me to take care of my children during the school week, attend meetings with the teachers, and help them with their school homework and assignments.

As had happened with my previous job, the paranoia returned. I wanted to return to the working world, in order to feel productive, as many people often make one feel. Regardless, the paranoia reared up its ugly head. I asked the Lord many times to heal me from it, and each time, he pointed me toward a passage with the apostle Paul. Paul says that three different times he asked the Lord to remove the thorn in his flesh, and each time the Lord's answer had been the same: to rejoice in his infirmity, because in his weakness, the Lord would be glorified (2 Corinthians 12:9 NIV).

After seeing I was unable to keep working, I busied myself visiting my mother as often as I could. Although she was not the same as her former being, I derived great comfort in seeing her. When the migraines would not allow it, my sister went, accompanied by my husband. I loved to stroke her forehead and kiss her hands, which were now papery soft. Losing her felt as though a part of my heart had been ripped out. I really do believe it was Jesus who gave me the courage and will to go on and to care for my young daughter and my sister, who is developmentally disabled.

My moment of fire came one afternoon when I was driving home with my daughter. I was close to the exit ramp, as I would be going in it shortly. As I passed the corner of a gas station, a car cut me off from the passenger's side, and I veered sharply to the right. My car went through the air, between two poles that held the name of the gas station, which I never saw. My car jumped the hedge with plants and soil where the two poles were placed and landed on the ground with one tire opening like a cracked nut. My husband went by the gas station the following day and measured the distance between the poles. It was the exact distance necessary for my car to go through.

I underwent through my fair share of heckling and derision from other people for saying I had not seen the poles. They took it to mean I thought of myself as special. The one reality was that I saw that in some way I could not explain, our lives had been saved. My daughter's infectious joy was a great relief amid difficult situations.

I yearned for my mother's presence and felt devastated by her loss. I was expected to carry on and get used to it. This, by no means, was easy. Three months before my mother passed, my son had left for the army. I felt a huge feeling of loss, with two of the people I loved the most gone. My daughter's presence was a balm for my bruised soul. Although I had not managed to make friends with other women, other than my sister's homemaker, who has been a true blessing to us, I was able to see the uplifting joy my daughter had and felt gladness. Her sweetness, and a maturity that was well beyond her years, helped me to withstand the distress of my mother's death and my son's absence.

In yet another effort to work, I undertook the study of public health. Having completed that, I have tried to find a job but have not been able to obtain one. I have placed the work search and continuing financial shortcomings in the Lord's hands. My marriage is still a troubled relationship. I feel much loneliness, but it is in these circumstances that the presence of Jesus shines the most. I have learned to depend on him, and that this is not a sign of weakness; giving him control makes our faith stronger.

Jesus has taught me to see my life through the gift of grace. My daughter has grown to be a beautiful young lady who in a year and a half will be graduating from high school. My son has finished serving in the army and continues to follow Jesus, and he is a focused young man who has gone on to study and is starting a life of his own.

Jesus has taught me one of the hardest lessons for me to learn. I cannot depend on other people for love and companionship but must keep my eyes fixed on him.

This does not mean that having friends is a bad thing. On the contrary, it is a blessing. But the source of our greatest trust and love must be the Lord. As years have passed, I have also become vocal about my illness, and this has sparked a desire to break the stigma against mental illness that continues to linger in our society, although it is not as pervasive as it was when I first became ill. This is a labor of love together with bringing the message of Jesus to other people.

I undertook writing this book as a testimony and for it to say about God's story and my own story. The two, interwoven, are a testimony of his power. The way I was drawn back to the faith and have been able to remain steadily serving him shows me the depth of his love. We are not alone when Jesus is with us. This book has been the culmination of a long-held dream; however, it being God's story and my story is a result of my participation in the Flourish Writers Program, led by two amazing Christian women, Jennifer Kochart and Mindy Kiker.

Before I became a part of this group, I had planned to write a book primarily focused on mental illness and overcoming the stigma, since it is so important to me for it to be broken. God's plan, however, was much more complete. I have been able to testify of the work of Jesus in my life. My rendering of this story is God's way of using my love for writing and putting it to a higher use than would have been served by my story only. Writing this book has been one of my greatest achievements. To be able to tell others about the incomparable love of Jesus and the story of redemption is an honor, a duty, and a great joy. To know that other people may read these lines and learn about the might of the Lord, about his love and peace that pass all understanding, is more than I ever dreamed of. It has been a great task and a tribute to the grace and love of Jesus, which knows no boundaries.

PART 2

H is ways are mysterious and higher than ours (Isaiah 55:9 NIV-MIT), the scriptures tell us. He has plans for our lives that unfold little by little. He does this, I believe, so we may understand that he has a time to do things, and this is intimately connected with his perfect will for our lives and the lives of those around us. His will and our journey are inextricably united. Nothing that happens in our lives is a coincidence. He looks for ways to teach us and prune us.

The season for pruning may feel very painful, but it is a necessary one. Just as it happens with plants, the pruning clears away unwanted matter. It teaches us to wait, a valuable trait, because patience comes hard to many of us. We live in an age when things happen at the touch of a button and wishes seem to be granted as we speak. But for the Christian journey, this is not so. What we ask for we need to wait in the Lord to receive. Some things, such as an urgent prayer for someone's life or salvation, are instantly answered. But for the most part, we must learn to wait.

This for me is particularly difficult, but I know that it is part of his shaping my character. A word he gave me— "Be still and know that I am God" (Psalm 46:10 NIV)—is an example. For me, being still is difficult. I long for quick, peremptory action for the things I want, need, or pray for. He tells me to be still. Because we are living in an era when things move very rapidly, we tend to assume that speed is paramount. But when God is forging our character, he does so in a way that is careful and measured. He wants us to learn his way and not that of the world we live in.

The constant rush we live in, going from one place to the next, is characteristic of this century. Most houses, at least the houses of those with wealth, have electronic gadgets like Alexa. In comparison to the twentieth century when I grew up, this is very strange. We cannot make time go back. We cannot change those things that trouble us about this way of life. We must keep track of the way we live, offering praises to our Lord throughout the day and thanking him for his goodness and care. Slowing down the pace we are moving at. Taking time to pray, praise, and adore. Recognize all the bounties he has for us, and thank him for his mercy. One thing that is very important is to learn how to manage our rollercoasters. By that I mean to manage our ups and downs, moments that are not necessarily easy to find but that we need to make the most out of. Slowing down the hurried pace. Looking to find time to think, reflect, and replenish ourselves. The Lord is always there, waiting for us to meet him. He urges us to find time for prayer, praise, and adoration. This is vitally important.

When we praise and adore the Lord, heavenly happenings occur. Our adoration opens the doors to miracles, to holy intervention in our everyday lives. When we have problems especially, praise and adoration are declarations of our trust in God. We recognize that his wisdom surpasses ours and that he has prepared works for us to complete. It also brings a special intimacy to our relationship with the Lord. It allows bonds of trust and joy to be deepened and is a manifestation that we are worshipping him as our Lord and Savior.

His ways are mysterious and fathomless (Romans 11:12 NIV-MIT). We do not know the reason for things to happen as they do, but our continued praise and thanksgiving are ways of acknowledging that whatever he allows to happen in our lives is for our best. He is Almighty. We are redeemed by the blood of the Lord Jesus. Trusting him in our most difficult moments refines our faith. It shows our complete surrender to his mighty will and power.

The Lord leads us "to rest by tranquil waters" (Psalm 23:2 NIV-MIT). In places of "green pastures" (Psalm 23:2 NIV-MIT), we may lie down and rest. He is our shield and buckler (Psalm 91:4 NIV-MIT). We shall not be abandoned or left defenseless. He gives his angels charge over us, that they may carry us and have our foot not stumble upon stones (Psalm 91:11 NIV-MIT). Above all, we must recognize that the life we have chosen, the life of faith, makes us forever children of the kingdom. Jesus ransomed us when he shed his holy blood and cleansed us of our sins.

Because of that, because he has enveloped us in his righteousness, we can enter the splendor of holiness (Psalm 29:2 NIV-MIT), where he and the Father and the Holy Spirit dwell and bow at the foot of the throne of grace in adoration. This is a great privilege that we cannot take for granted. When we sin, we must repent, confess our sin, and ask for forgiveness that we may be restored. Our task is to walk in the Spirit and let others know about the good news, the hope to which we have been called. The Spirit himself intercedes for us with groans (Romans 8:26 KJV) that express that which we cannot say, and that is because he knows the mind of God (Romans 8:27 KJV), as Paul tells us in his epistles.

Because we are children of the kingdom, we must realize that our body is the temple of the Holy Spirit (1 Corinthians 16:19 KJV). That means we must honor God with our bodies, and that is why we must keep it free from sin. Because we live in a fallen world, there always is going to be sin in our surroundings and ourselves. But when we commit a sin, we must ask God to forgive us and restore us before his sight. Our mission is to let others know about Christ, and that includes letting them see Christ in us.

In many instances, we are tempted to do, say, or see things that would bring sin into our lives. Sometimes we will fail to be as trustworthy as he deems us to be. But at all times, our focus should be to walk in the Spirit, so the connection between our Lord and us may always be in place. Paul, in his epistles to the churches, said, "What connection can there be between believers and unbelievers, holiness and sin" (2 Corinthians 6:15 NLT). His meaning rings true, especially in our era, because he says there is to be no union between the unbeliever and the believer.

One thing that is sometimes difficult to do is to keep our will subject to the will of the Lord Jesus. Because we have been given the freedom to choose, doing as we wish will sometimes—*many* times—be desirable to us. But Paul warns about this very thing. His word to the churches was that "our body is the temple of the Holy Spirit. If we destroy our bodies, the Spirit will destroy us" (1 Corinthians 6:19 NIV). How do we destroy our bodies? Using drugs is one example. Getting drunk. Having sexual relationships outside marriage.

Scriptures say in the gospels by the apostles, the book of Revelation, the epistles of Paul, as well as in the Old Testament, that the church is the bride of Christ. As such, it must be kept free from sin and worldly affairs. We, as Christians, must preserve the holiness of Jesus and not defile our bodies by doing things that will cause it damage or sinfulness. Our society is so indifferent to Christ that these things may appear normal to us, but in fact they are not. I will use Samson, looking into the Old Testament, as an example. He was gifted by God with extraordinary strength. Samson was consecrated as a Nazarene, something which is explained in the book of Numbers (Numbers 6:1–21 NIV-MIT). The secret of his strength was that he should never cut his hair.

However, then he fell in love with Delilah, a foreign woman. Although he had been warned to never reveal his secret, he told her. She waited until he slept and cut off his hair. Then men of her people came and defeated him, without his strength. He was taken to a temple where the people gathered. His prayer to God was to let him die with them, as time had passed and his hair had grown. Samson stood between the columns of the temple, held each one, and then collapsed them to the ground, killing more of these enemies of Israel than he ever had before (Judges 16:4–28 GNB).

We see this also happen to King Solomon. When asked by God what he desired, he asked for wisdom. He was the wisest man on earth (1 Kings 3:5–9 GNB). God forewarned him not to take foreign wives, for they would lead his heart astray. He, however, did take them, despite God's warning. As a consequence, his heart went wayward and he worshipped pagan idols (1 Kings 11:1–5 GNB). God removed him from the throne of Israel, and he met his death.

To better understand the analogy of the church being the bride of Christ, let us look at human marriages. Each partner expects to have sexual fidelity, to have their income spent on the home's needs, and the wishes of each of them, to be told the truth by their spouse in all things that concern the marriage. When one of the spouses deviates from this, the other one feels betrayal, disrespect, and lack of commitment to the marriage. In our society, even though we live in a fallen world, these things are still expected of the married couple.

God's expectations of us are not unrealistic. When we give our hearts to Jesus and ask him to be our Lord, we are expected to surrender to him as our Lord and Savior. Engaging in behavior that is sinful is a sign of betrayal of our Lord, the betrayal of our faith. We are in effect telling God that we are going to exercise our free will and live according to our wishes. He will not stop us as he gave us free will, and that means we are free to choose what we want to do.

However, unless we repent and ask for forgiveness, our relationship with the Lord will have been broken. Once this happens, we become children of disobedience, and that will dictate the way we live . We will commit more sinful acts, fall deeper into disobedience, and get farther from God and deeper into sin. All the mistakes we make will dictate the way our life unfolds and the problems we may encounter. We will face all risks and difficulties on our own. The most dangerous thing is that our hearts will become hardened against God. The further we fall into sin, the harder our hearts will become, and we will be less and less willing to repent.

Because we are defiling the temple of the Holy Spirit, our reasoning and intentions will not be aligned with God's will. By rejecting the presence of the Lord in our lives, we become easy prey to the enemy of our soul. He will be able to have more and more control over us and our lives. This is what happened to Saul, the king who preceded David in the throne of Israel. Saul saw that David had the anointing of the Holy Spirit, and he sought to kill him. Saul was faithless because the Spirit of the Lord had abandoned him, and the Lord had allowed a messenger from Satan to cause him pain and restlessness (1 Samuel 18:6–20, 42 NRSEB).

There are many instances in our lives when situations will come up that will test us. We may feel inclined to do something that gives us pleasure but is against God's will. In these instances, we must go to the scriptures and seek an answer from the Lord about what to do. Our prayers will also enable us to discern between truth and falsehood. At no time can we allow ourselves to separate from God's will because of what this implies for our relationship with the Lord.

Temptations may come in many ways, and sometimes we will be unable to recognize what they mean. Maybe they will not be easy to spot. Maybe it will be an action or a thought that unravels a series of behaviors. When we become aware of this, at any stage, we need to go before the Lord and bow before his great majesty and repent. Jesus will intercede for us before the Father, and the Spirit will come back to us with his anointing.

This is a great and marvelous truth. God will forgive us if we truly repent. Walking with Jesus means walking in the Spirit. Searching in the scriptures for the daily words of nourishment that our souls need. It takes effort, but it is not wasted effort. The relationship between Jesus and us is the most wonderful relationship we will ever have.

This means knowing that we and those we love, and those we pray for, are under the Lord's protection. Seeing our prayers answered without us having to do something huge to receive this blessing. Paul told the churches that we are in grace, and this is a gift from God, not something we can earn, so no one can take from God's glory (Ephesians 2:8–9 KJV).

Walking with Jesus means walking in grace. Seeing and experiencing miraculous circumstances happening as a matter of course. Being witness to the majesty of the Lord and bearing the fruits of the Spirit, and if we see that we do not have all of them, asking, humbly and with constancy, that the Spirit may do the necessary work in our lives. It may be a difficult work sometimes. In fact, Jesus said to his disciples, "In the world you will have trouble, but fear not, because I have overcome the world" (John 16:33 KJV). This tells us that we can expect to encounter difficult circumstances, but if we bring them before the Lord, he shall see us through them.

This is a promise, not a threat. We will encounter trouble but need not fear because in rising from the dead, he overcame death and the troubles of this world. In another part of the scriptures, Jesus says, "I will be with you until the end" (Matthew 28:20 NKJV). He said this to his disciples after he had risen and appeared to them as they were assembled, and this was his promise. Only he can make this promise. With his resurrection, he was given a name above all names and was made worthy of all praise.

God upholds us with his right hand. He lifts us up from our difficulties and takes care of our being. He takes care of our physical and spiritual needs. We are safe in the One who loves us. And in return, we worship him. One important aspect of worship, which cannot be overlooked, is taking all idolatry out of our lives. God clearly shows, both in the Old Testament and New Testament, that he will not tolerate his children worshipping other idols (Exodus 34:14 NASB).

These idols may not necessarily be pagan gods, as we would assume, but material possessions, people, ambitions, and goals that we have and may not be willing to give up. The scriptures say that our God "is a consuming fire" (Hebrews 12:29 KJV). He alone reigns, and he will not tolerate us turning to other idols, doing things that we he does not want us to do, and giving entrance in our bodies to a sinful presence. He can see inside of our hearts and knows what we are planning to do or want to do. Our thoughts and actions must be in accord with his will, so we may be led and blessed.

Disobeying God is not something to be taken lightly. His mercy is great, but so is his wrath. Above all, we must remember he is holy. The psalmist says, "Those with clean hands and pure hearts, who have not known deceit" (Psalm 24:1–6 NKJV), when speaking about who would be allowed to enter the dwelling place of the Most High.

Elsewhere, the psalmist says, "Adore God in the beauty of Holiness" (Psalm 96:9 NIV). That tells us how sacred God is. A holy presence.

We must be aware of the holiness of God and abide in that knowledge. Jesus said the Father was looking for those who would adore him in Spirit and in Truth. This is a big endeavor. In order to fulfill this, we must walk in the Spirit, which correlates living the life that Jesus expects of us as his saved, redeemed, and loyal disciples. Our lives as Christians must be looked at in the framework of our relationship with God.

Our daily practice of prayer, praise, and studying the scriptures underscores the deep necessity to walk in the Spirit, letting our Lord dictate our actions, motives, thoughts, and plans. It makes no sense to plan without first bringing it to God in prayer. Is this his will? Is this what he wants and would have us do? Often, in our walk with Jesus, we encounter many difficulties. Again I underscore this. Jesus told his disciples, "In the world you shall have trouble. But fear not, I have overcome the world" (John 16:33 KJV).

This word must be noted: "overcome." Jesus has overcome the world, defeated death, and resurrected so that we may be ransomed for our sins. In another passage, the Lord tells us, "Be still and know that I am God" (Psalm 46:10 NIV). In this case, the emphasis is on the word "stillness." Here we have two different concepts: overcome and stillness. How can these two words work together? First, we must be aware that we alone cannot overcome. It is by the power of the Holy Spirit that we overcome obstacles.

Second, the Lord tells us to be still. Why? Because we have this command: to wait in stillness for the Lord to act. God has his own time in which he acts. And our task is to be still and wait. Trying to figure out how we can use these two words in our Christian living, we are faced with one reality: it is God who can do things on our behalf, not us. We must be obedient, pray, wait, and be still, allowing the Lord to act in our circumstances.

In our walk with Jesus, we encounter this situation many times. It is hard to wait. It is even harder to be still. Our very nature opposes this thought. We are raised to act, to become, and to overcome. But the Lord wants us to learn to wait upon his time. This is illustrated in the passage in the scriptures when Jesus is apprehended. When this occurred, he told his disciples, "Do you not know that I can call upon my Father for help?" (Matthew 26:53 KJV). The fact that Jesus kept silent and went, as scriptures say, "as a lamb to be slaughtered" (Isaiah 53:7 NIV) tells us very clearly that his is the example we must follow.

Jesus knew he could summon hosts of angels to rescue him, but he did not do this. He had been given a task by the Father, and he was going to fulfill that mission. He knew only his death could ransom us. He suffered incredible and horrifying pain in a physical body so he could fulfill his purpose. His eyes were fixed on the Father and on the task ahead. Therefore, he was silent when he was interrogated. He was silent when he was whipped and a crown of thorns was placed on his head. His silence is the equivalent of our stillness. If we are his disciples, we are to follow his footsteps.

When Jesus spoke to the disciples about the burdens that people carry, he said, "Bring me your burden and take mine. Because mine is light and easy to carry" (Matthew 11:28–30 AMP). He had warned them that in the world they would suffer persecution and betrayal in his name. But the Word he gave them was this: "I will be with you every day until the end" (Matthew 28:20 NKJV). Ours is not a heavy taskmaster. He gives us work that needs to be done—the work of the kingdom. That work is accomplished through the Spirit who empowers us and gives us the words to say. Scriptures say that the Spirit would guide us to all truth, because he knows the mind of God. The Spirit is the One who intercedes for us with "moans and groans, utterances that cannot be explained" (Romans 8:26 KJV), for he is praying for our liberation, for our victory over sin, and over the works of darkness because we have been ransomed by the blood of the Lamb.

It is a great joy to follow Jesus. It is a great honor that we were lost in our sinful lives and he redeemed us by shedding his precious blood and resurrecting from the grave. The same Spirit that raised Jesus from the grave is the Spirit that we carry with us. That is why scriptures say,

"Our body is the temple of the Holy Spirit" (1 Corinthians 6:19 KJV). Walking with Jesus requires of us obedience, reverence, and love—the love that he put into our hearts. Love for his ways and for his word. For his church, which is everywhere around the world and which shall be raised by him as he returns for his bride. In his epistles to the churches, Paul tells us that the church is the bride of Jesus.

We are a "holy people, a nation of priests" (1 Peter 2:9 NIV), a people God has called into himself, and Jesus, in redeeming us, cleansed us from our sin and gave us eternal life. In one of the psalms, David says, "From the womb of my mother, you called me by name" (Galatians 1:15 NIV). Paul says, "We are to fulfill the holy works which He has prepared for us" (Ephesians 2:10 NIV). Our presence on the earth is that which keeps the enemy from ruling over people's lives and carrying out his works of destruction and damnation.

It is my greatest desire that if someone is reading this book and does not know the Lord Jesus as their Savior, they may pause and consider what the meaning of this story is; they may also be able to know Jesus as their Lord and Savior, bow their heads and their hearts, and say a simple prayer—but a most important one.

> Jesus, I want to repent from my sins and receive you as my Lord. Come into my heart and make your abode in me. Let your Holy Spirit come into my life and guide me

to know and follow the will of the Father. Give me a desire to read your Word so I may be able to learn more about you and your Father and about the fruits of the Spirit. Thank you, Jesus, for listening to me and answering my prayer. Amen.

NOTES

Printed in the United States
by Baker & Taylor Publisher Services